Claim *the*
promises
of
GOD
and Prepare for a
Miracle

Revised Edition

Rev. Harris D. McFarlane

Published By Cornerstone Publishing
info@thecornerstonepublishers.com
www.thecornerstonepublishers.com

CONTACT INFORMATION

To order bulk copies of this book, please send email to:

info@dimensionministries.org

365 Promises:
One for Each
Day of the Year

Introduction

I want to implore you to base your life on the promises of God. The promises of God will never let you down. Human promises are often broken. Resolutions don't last. Goals are often not accomplished. Human plans will many times be changed. But the promises of God will never fail. God in his awesome power, love, grace, and truth has created for us the opportunity to reunite with Him and live the life He has ordained and planned for us from the beginning through his magnificent and precious promises.

Don't be afraid to step out into the dimensions of tomorrow for God will be with you always through the numerous promises that he has made over 3,000 years ago to us. These promises are at the forefront and center of God's heart. He wants us to know them, claim them, live by them, so we can have breakthroughs, victories, and miracles in our lives. If you want more wisdom, it begins with God's promises. If you want more faith, it begins with God's promises. If you want more peace, it begins with God's promises. If you want more hope, it begins with God's promises. If you want more power, it begins with God's promises.

How do you live a life of Faith? You choose to live by the promises of God. When you live a life that is based on the promises of God, you're living a very powerful life because faith unlocks all the promises of God.

What is faith?

Paul said, "Faith is the substance of things hoped for: the evidence of things not seen." Augustine said, "For what is faith unless it is to believe what you don't see?" Faith is like the seeds you deposit in the ground: you cannot see them, but when you cherish, water, fertilize, and nurture them, they will grow exponentially.

God always keeps His amazing promises. You can trust, depend, and lean on God's promises. Several spectacular examples of God's promises are illustrated in the following scriptures:

Let us hold fast the profession of our faith without wavering (for he is faithful that promised). (Hebrew 10:23)

For verily I say unto you, That whosoever shall say unto this mountain, Be thou removed, and be thou cast into the sea; and shall not doubt in his heart, but shall believe that those things which he saith shall come to pass; he shall have whatsoever he saith. (Mark 11:23)

You were made to rise above all worries, fear, obstacles and emanate the can do attitude. I can do all things through Christ which strengtheneth me. (Philippians 4:13)

And what shall I more say? For the time would fail me to tell of Gedeon, and of Barak, and of Samson, and of Jephthae; of David also, and Samuel, and of the prophets:

Who through faith subdued kingdoms, wrought righteousness, obtained promises, stopped the mouths of lions. Quenched the violence of fire, escaped the edge of the sword, out of weakness were made strong, waxed valiant in fight, turned to fight the armies of the aliens. (Hebrews 11:32-34)

I encourage you to get your eyes off the mountains and focus your eyes on the promises of God. Start decreeing and say, "God, I am not going to settle for less than I can be anymore. I am ready to move mountains and start living only by your promises." With this attitude and conviction, God always shows up and performs a miracle.

We have to go beyond our imaginations, beyond our expectations, beyond our abilities, beyond our resources, beyond our talents, beyond our dreams and visions, beyond our walls, into the stratospheric promises of God, so we can transform and catapult our destiny.

There are thousands of promises in the bible ready to be claimed. Promises of peace, healing, success, strength, health, hope, wisdom, salvation, confidence, faith, prosperity, and many more. Why does God make these promises? Because he wants you to trust him, depend upon him and believe in him. God likes to use ordinary people to accomplish extraordinary things. Please join me in this life-changing journey as you rediscover your divine heritage of the promises of God. These promises will unleash and unfold miracles in your life.

These 365 promises, one for each day of the year, initiate a breathtaking journey that will transform, renew, and elevate your life to new dimensions. Seize the moment for this extraordinary journey to fulfilling your life's purpose.

This is not a substitute for the Bible. It is a reminder, guide, and direction to some of the most amazing promises taken from the King James Version (KJV) of the Bible.

I wish every reader an awakening, transformation, elevation, breakthrough, and many miracles in your spiritual, emotional, mental, social, economic, personal, relational, and physical life.

"I am come that they might have life, and that they might have it more abundantly." (John 10:10)

1. "Call unto me, and I will answer thee, and show thee great and mighty things, which thou knowest not." (Jeremiah 33:3)

2. "Every good gift and every perfect gift is from above, and cometh down from the Father of lights, with whom is no variableness, neither shadow of turning." (James 1:17)

3. "The blessing of the Lord, it maketh rich, and he addeth no sorrow with it." (Proverbs 10:22)

4. "Therefore if any man be in Christ, he is a new creature: old things are passed away; behold all things are become new." (2 Corinthians 5:17)

5. "For I know the thoughts that I think toward you, saith the Lord, thoughts of peace and not of evil, to give you an expected end." (Jeremiah 29:11)

6. "Now unto him that is able to do exceeding abundantly above all that we ask or think, according to the power that worketh in us." (Ephesians 3:20)

7. "But without faith it is impossible to please him: for he that cometh to God must believe that he is and that he is a rewarder of them that diligently seek him." (Hebrews 11:6)

8. "The Lord is my shepherd; I shall not want." (Psalm 23:1)

9. "Beloved, I wish above all things that thou mayest prosper and be in health, even as thy soul prospereth." (3 John 1:2)

10. "The Lord is my light and my salvation; whom shall I fear? The Lord is the strength of my life; of whom shall I be afraid?." (Psalm 27:1)

11. "Verily, verily, I say unto you, He that believeth on me the works that I do shall he do also; and greater works than these shall he do; because I go unto my Father." (John 14:12)

12. "For the LORD God is a sun and shield: the LORD will give grace and glory: no good thing will he withhold from them that walk uprightly." (Psalm 84:11)

13. "Ask, and it shall be given you; seek, and ye shall find; knock, and it shall be opened unto you: for everyone that asketh receiveth; and he that seeketh findeth; and to him that knocketh it shall be opened." (Matthew 7:7-8)

14. "Know therefore that the LORD thy God, he is God, the faithful God, which keepeth covenant and mercy with them that love him and keep his commandments to a thousand generations." (Deuteronomy 7:9)

15. "But thou shalt remember the Lord thy God: for it is he that giveth thee power to get wealth, that he may establish his covenant which he sware unto thy fathers, as it is this day." (Deuteronomy 8:18)

16. "Bring ye all the tithes into the storehouse, that there may be meat in mine house, and prove me now herewith, saith the Lord of hosts, if I will not open you the windows of heaven, and pour you out a blessing, that there shall not be room enough to receive it." (Malachi 3:10)

17. "But this I say, 'He which soweth sparingly shall reap also sparingly; and he which soweth bountifully shall reap also bountifully'." (2 Corinthians 9:6)

18. "But seek ye first the kingdom of God, and his righteousness; and all these things shall be added unto you." (Matthew 6:33)

19. "Give, and it shall be given unto you; good measure, pressed down, and shaken together, and running over, shall men give into your bosom. For with the same measure that ye mete withal it shall be measured to you again." (Luke 6:38)

20. "For all the promises of God in him are yea, and in him Amen, unto the glory of God by us." (2 Corinthians 1:20)

21. "God is not a man that he should lie; neither the son of man that he should repent: hath he said, and shall he not do it? Or hath he spoken, and shall he not make it good?." (Numbers 23:19)

22. "² And all these blessings shall come on thee, and overtake thee, if thou shalt hearken unto the voice of the Lord thy God. ³ Blessed shalt thou be in the city, and blessed shalt thou be in the field. ⁴ Blessed shall be the fruit of thy body, and the fruit of thy ground, and the fruit of thy cattle, the increase of thy kine, and the flocks of thy sheep. ⁵ Blessed shall be thy basket and thy store. ⁶ Blessed shalt thou be when thou comest in, and blessed shalt thou be when thou goest out." (Deuteronomy 28:2-6)

23. "The Lord shall command the blessing upon thee in thy storehouses, and in all that thou settest thine hand unto; and he shall bless thee in the land which the Lord thy God giveth thee." (Deuteronomy 28:8)

24. "¹ Now the Lord had said unto Abram, 'Get thee out of thy country, and from thy kindred, and from thy father's house, unto a land that I will shew thee: ² And I will make of thee a great nation, and I will bless thee, and make thy name great; and thou shalt be a blessing: ³ And I will bless them that bless thee, and curse him that curseth thee: and in thee shall all families of the earth be blessed'." (Genesis 12:1-3)

25. "Whereby are given unto us exceeding great and precious promises: that by these ye might be partakers of the divine nature, having escaped the corruption that is in the world through lust." (2 Peter 1:4)

26. "And his master saw that the LORD was with him, and that the LORD made all that he did to prosper in his hand." (Genesis 39:3)

27. "The keeper of the prison looked not to anything that was under his hand; because the LORD was with him, and that which he did, the LORD made it to prosper." (Genesis 39:23)

28. "If the LORD delight in us, then he will bring us into this land, and give it us; a land which floweth with milk and honey." (Numbers 14:8)

29. "Only be thou strong and very courageous, that thou mayest observe to do according to all the law, which Moses my servant commanded thee: turn not from it to the right hand or to the left, that thou mayest prosper whithersoever thou goest." (Joshua 1:7)

30. "This book of the law shall not depart out of thy mouth; but thou shalt meditate therein day and night, that thou mayest observe to do according to all that is written therein: for then thou shalt make thy way prosperous, and then thou shalt have good success." (Joshua 1:8)

31. "The LORD maketh poor, and maketh rich: he bringeth low, and lifteth up." (1 Samuel 2:7)

32. "And keep the charge of the LORD thy God, to walk in his ways, to keep his statutes, and his commandments, and his judgments, and his testimonies, as it is written in the law of Moses, that thou mayest prosper in all that thou doest, and whithersoever thou turnest thyself." (1 Kings 2:3)

33. "Wisdom and knowledge is granted unto thee; and I will give thee riches, and wealth, and honour, such as none of the kings have had that have been before thee, neither shall there any after thee have the like." 2 Chronicles 1:12

34. "And they rose early in the morning, and went forth into the wilderness of Tekoa: and as they went forth, Jehoshaphat stood and said, 'Hear me, O Judah, and ye inhabitants of Jerusalem; Believe in the LORD your God, so shall ye be established; believe his prophets, so shall ye prosper.'" (2 Chronicles 20:20)

35. "And he sought God in the days of Zechariah, who had understanding in the visions of God: and as long as he sought the LORD, God made him to prosper." (2 Chronicles 26:5)

36. "For thou, Lord, wilt bless the righteous; with favour wilt thou compass him as with a shield." (Psalm 5:12)

37. "Thou preparest a table before me in the presence of mine enemies: thou anointest my head with oil; my cup runneth over." (Psalm 23:5)

38. "Surely goodness and mercy shall follow me all the days of my life: and I will dwell in the house of the Lord forever." (Psalm 23:6)

39. "The young lions do lack, and suffer hunger: but they that seek the LORD shall not want any good thing." (Psalm 34:10)

40. "Let them shout for joy, and be glad, that favour my righteous cause: yea, let them say continually, Let the Lord be magnified, which hath pleasure in the prosperity of his servant." (Psalm 35:27)

41. "And ye shall seek me, and find me, when ye shall search for me with all your heart." (Jeremiah 29:13)

42. "And if ye be Christ's, then are ye Abraham's seed, and heirs according to the promise." (Galatians 3:29)

43. "Blessed be the LORD, that hath given rest unto his people Israel, according to all that he promised: there hath not failed one word of all his good promise, which he promised by the hand of Moses his servant." (1 Kings 8:56)

44. "The angel of the LORD encampeth round about them that fear him, and delivereth them." (Psalm 34:7)

45. "He shall cover thee with his feathers, and under his wings shalt thou trust: his truth shall be thy shield and buckler." (Psalm 91:4)

46. "The LORD your God which goeth before you, he shall fight for you, according to all that he did for you in Egypt before your eyes." (Deuteronomy 1:30)

47. "The LORD bless thee, and keep thee." (Numbers 6:24)

48. "Behold, I give unto you power to tread on serpents and scorpions, and over all the power of the enemy: and nothing shall by any means hurt you." (Luke 10:19)

49. "For I will pour water upon him that is thirsty, and floods upon the dry ground: I will pour my spirit upon thy seed, and my blessing upon thine offspring." (Isaiah 44:3)

50. "For I am the LORD, I change not; therefore ye sons of Jacob are not consumed." (Malachi 3:6)

51. "For this God is our God forever and ever: he will be our guide even unto death." (Psalm 48:14)

52. "Thou art my hiding place; thou shalt preserve me from trouble; thou shalt compass me about with songs of deliverance. Selah." (Psalm 32:7)

53. "Cast thy burden upon the LORD, and he shall sustain thee: he shall never suffer the righteous to be moved." (Psalm 55:22)

54. "He that spared not his own Son, but delivered him up for us all, how shall he not with him also freely give us all things?." (Romans 8:32)

55. "Give us this day our daily bread." (Matthew 6:11)

56. "Blessed are the poor in spirit: for theirs is the kingdom of heaven." (Matthew 5:3)

57. "But thou, when thou prayest, enter into thy closet, and when thou hast shut thy door, pray to thy Father which is in secret; and thy Father which seeth in secret shall reward thee openly." (Matthew 6:6)

58. "Before I formed thee in the belly I knew thee; and before thou camest forth out of the womb I sanctified thee, and I ordained thee a prophet unto the nations." (Jeremiah 1:5)

59. "And, behold, this day I am going the way of all the earth: and ye know in all your hearts and in all your souls, that not one thing hath failed of all the good things which the Lord your God spake concerning you; all are come to pass unto you, and not one thing hath failed thereof." (Joshua 23:14)

60. "Nay, in all these things we are more than conquerors through him that loved us." (Romans 8:37)

61. "There hath no temptation taken you but such as is common to man: but God is faithful, who will not suffer you to be tempted above that ye are able; but will with the temptation also make a way to escape, that ye may be able to bear it." (1 Corinthians 10:13)

62. "Casting all your care upon him; for he careth for you." (1 Peter 5:7)

63. "For God so loved the world, that he gave his only begotten Son, that whosoever believeth in him should not perish, but have everlasting life." (John 3:16)

64. "He only is my rock and my salvation; he is my defense; I shall not be greatly moved." (Psalm 62:2)

65. "Thy mercy, O Lord, is in the heavens; and thy faithfulness reacheth unto the clouds." (Psalm 36:5)

66. "Blessed is the man that endureth temptation: for when he is tried, he shall receive the crown of life, which the Lord hath promised to them that love him." (James 1:12)

67. "Delight thyself also in the L*ord*: and he shall give thee the desires of thine heart." (Psalm 37:4)

68. "Blessed is that man that maketh the L*ord* his trust, and respecteth not the proud, nor such as turn aside to lies." (Psalm 40:4)

69. "Thou hast caused men to ride over our heads; we went through fire and through water: but thou broughtest us out into a wealthy place." (Psalm 66:12)

70. "But verily God hath heard me; he hath attended to the voice of my prayer." (Psalm 66:19)

71. "Blessed is the man whose strength is in thee; in whose heart are the ways of them." (Psalm 84:5)

72. "And he increased his people greatly; and made them stronger than their enemies." (Psalm 105:24)

73. "He brought them forth also with silver and gold: and there was not one feeble person among their tribes." (Psalm 105:37)

74. "Praise ye the LORD. Blessed is the man that feareth the LORD, that delighteth greatly in his commandments." (Psalm 112:1)

75. "Wealth and riches shall be in his house: and his righteousness endureth for ever." (Psalm 112:3)

76. "He will bless them that fear the LORD, both small and great." (Psalm 115:13)

77. "The LORD shall increase you more and more, you and your children." (Psalm 115:14)

78. "Return unto thy rest, O my soul; for the LORD hath dealt bountifully with thee." (Psalm 116:7)

79. "Save now, I beseech thee, O Lord: O Lord, I beseech thee, send now prosperity." (Psalm 118:25)

80. "Blessed are they that keep his testimonies, and that seek him with the whole heart." (Psalm 119:2)

81. "Peace be within thy walls and prosperity within thy palaces." (Psalm 122:7)

82. "Blessed is every one that feareth the Lord; that walketh in his ways." (Psalm 128:1)

83. "For thou shalt eat the labour of thine hands: happy shalt thou be, and it shall be well with thee." (Psalm 128:2)

84. "⁹ Honour the Lord with thy substance, and with the first fruits of all thine increase. ¹⁰ So shall thy barns be filled with plenty, and thy presses shall burst out with new wine." (Proverbs 3:9-10)

85. "The curse of the LORD is in the house of the wicked: but he blesseth the habitation of the just." (Proverbs 3:33)

86. "That I may cause those that love me to inherit substance; and I will fill their treasures." (Proverbs 8:21)

87. "He becometh poor that dealeth with a slack hand: but the hand of the diligent maketh rich." (Proverbs 10:4)

88. "⁶ Blessings are upon the head of the just: but violence covereth the mouth of the wicked. ⁷ The memory of the just is blessed: but the name of the wicked shall rot." (Proverbs 10:6-7)

89. "A gracious woman retaineth honour: and strong men retain riches." (Proverbs 11:16)

90. "The liberal soul shall be made fat: and he that watereth shall be watered also himself." (Proverbs 11:25)

91. "Wealth gotten by vanity shall be diminished: but he that gathereth by labour shall increase." (Proverbs 13:11)

92. "A good man leaveth an inheritance to his children's children: and the wealth of the sinner is laid up for the just." (Proverbs 13:22)

93. "In the house of the righteous is much treasure: but in the revenues of the wicked is trouble." (Proverbs 15:6)

94. "Commit thy works unto the LORD, and thy thoughts shall be established." (Proverbs 16:3)

95. "⁶ Be careful for nothing; but in everything by prayer and supplication with thanksgiving let your requests be made known unto God. ⁷And the peace of God, which passeth all understanding, shall keep your hearts and minds through Christ Jesus. ⁸ Finally, brethren, whatsoever things are true, whatsoever things are honest, whatsoever things are just, whatsoever things are pure, whatsoever things are lovely, whatsoever things are of good report; if there be any virtue, and if there be any praise, think on these things. ⁹ Those things, which ye have both learned, and received, and heard, and seen in me, do: and the God of peace shall be with you." (Philippians 4:6-9)

96. "I can do all things through Christ which strengtheneth me." (Philippians 4:13)

97. "I have been young, and now am old; yet have I not seen the righteous forsaken, nor his seed begging bread." (Psalm 37:25)

98. "And said, 'If thou wilt diligently hearken to the voice of the LORD thy God, and wilt do that which is right in his sight, and wilt give ear to his commandments, and keep all his statutes, I will put none of these diseases upon thee, which I have brought upon the Egyptians: for I am the LORD that healeth thee'." (Exodus 15:26)

99. "⁵ Trust in the LORD with all thine heart; and lean not unto thine own understanding. ⁶ In all thy ways acknowledge him, and he shall direct thy paths. ⁷ Be not wise in thine own eyes: fear the LORD, and depart from evil. ⁸ It shall be health to thy navel, and marrow to thy bones." (Proverbs 3:5-8)

100. "²⁰ My son, attend to my words; incline thine ear unto my sayings. ²¹ Let them not depart from thine eyes; keep them in the midst of thine heart. ²² For they are life unto those that find them, and health to all their flesh. ²³ Keep thy heart with all diligence; for out of it are the issues of life." (Proverbs 4:20-23)

101. "Heal me, O Lord, and I shall be healed; save me, and I shall be saved: for thou art my praise." (Jeremiah 17:14)

102. "'For I will restore health unto thee, and I will heal thee of thy wounds,' saith the Lord; 'because they called thee an outcast, saying, This is Zion, whom no man seeketh after'." (Jeremiah 30:17)

103. "Behold, I will bring it health and cure, and I will cure them, and will reveal unto them the abundance of peace and truth." (Jeremiah 33:6)

104. "And when he had called unto him his twelve disciples, he gave them power against unclean spirits, to cast them out, and to heal all manner of sickness and all manner of disease." (Matthew 10:1)

105. "And he said unto her, 'Daughter, thy faith hath made thee whole; go in peace, and be whole of thy plague'." (Mark 5:34)

106. "And the people, when they knew it, followed him: and he received them, and spake unto them of the kingdom of God, and healed them that had need of healing." (Luke 9:11)

107. "[14] Is any sick among you? Let him call for the elders of the church; and let them pray over him, anointing him with oil in the name of the Lord: [15] And the prayer of faith shall save the sick, and the Lord shall raise him up; and if he have committed sins, they shall be forgiven him. [16] Confess your faults one to another, and pray one for another, that ye may be healed. The effectual fervent prayer of a righteous man availeth much." (James 5:14-16)

108. "Fear thou not; for I am with thee: be not dismayed; for I am thy God: I will strengthen thee; yea, I will help thee; yea, I will uphold thee with the right hand of my righteousness." (Isaiah 41:10)

109. "'For the mountains shall depart, and the hills be removed; but my kindness shall not depart from thee, neither shall the covenant of my peace be removed,' saith the LORD that hath mercy on thee." (Isaiah 54:10)

110. "But the mercy of the LORD is from everlasting to everlasting upon them that fear him, and his righteousness unto children's children." (Psalm 103:17)

111. "The LORD shall fight for you, and ye shall hold your peace." (Exodus 14:14)

112. "And the LORD, he it is that doth go before thee; he will be with thee, he will not fail thee, neither forsake thee: fear not, neither be dismayed." (Deuteronomy 31:8)

113. "Have not I commanded thee? Be strong and of a good courage; be not afraid, neither be thou dismayed: for the LORD thy God is with thee whithersoever thou goest." (Joshua 1:9)

114. "For thou hast been a shelter for me, and a strong tower from the enemy." (Psalm 61:3)

115. "For I the LORD thy God will hold thy right hand, saying unto thee, Fear not; I will help thee." (Isaiah 41:13)

116. "When thou passest through the waters, I will be with thee; and through the rivers, they shall not overflow thee: when thou walkest through the fire, thou shalt not be burned; neither shall the flame kindle upon thee." (Isaiah 43:2)

117. "Peace I leave with you, my peace I give unto you: not as the world giveth, give I unto you. Let not your heart be troubled, neither let it be afraid." (John 14:27)

118. "¹³ And whatsoever ye shall ask in my name, that will I do, that the Father may be glorified in the Son. ¹⁴ If ye shall ask any thing in my name, I will do it. ¹⁵ If ye love me, keep my commandments. ¹⁶ And I will pray the Father, and he shall give you another Comforter, that he may abide with you forever." (John 14:13-16)

119. "But ye shall receive power, after that the Holy Ghost is come upon you: and ye shall be witnesses unto me both in Jerusalem, and in all Judaea, and in Samaria, and unto the uttermost part of the earth." (Acts 1:8)

120. "³¹ Therefore take no thought, saying, 'What shall we eat? or, What shall we drink? or, Wherewithal shall we be clothed?' ³² (For after all these things do the Gentiles seek:) for your heavenly Father knoweth that ye have need of all these things. (Matthew 6:31-32)

121. "If my people, which are called by my name, shall humble themselves, and pray, and seek my face, and turn from their wicked ways; then will I hear from heaven, and will forgive their sin, and will heal their land." (2 Chronicles 7:14)

122. "And, behold, I am with thee, and will keep thee in all places whither thou goest, and will bring thee again into this land; for I will not leave thee, until I have done that which I have spoken to thee of." (Genesis 28:15)

123. "If any of you lack wisdom, let him ask of God, that giveth to all men liberally, and upbraideth not; and it shall be given him." (James 1:5)

124. "And Jesus saith unto him, I will come and heal him." (Matthew 8:7)

125. "² Speak ye comfortably to Jerusalem, and cry unto her, that her warfare is accomplished, that her iniquity is pardoned: for she hath received of the LORD's hand double for all her sins. ³ The voice of him that crieth in the wilderness, Prepare ye the way of the LORD, make straight in the desert a highway for our God. ⁴ Every valley shall be exalted, and every mountain and hill shall be made low: and the crooked shall be made straight, and the rough places plain: ⁵ And the glory of the LORD shall be revealed, and all flesh shall see it together: for the mouth of the LORD hath spoken it." (Isaiah 40:2-5)

126. "¹⁰ The LORD your God hath multiplied you, and, behold, you are this day as the stars of heaven for multitude. ¹¹ (The LORD God of your fathers make you a thousand times so many more as ye are, and bless you, as he hath promised you!)." (Deuteronomy 1:10-11)

127. "³⁸ For I am persuaded, that neither death, nor life, nor angels, nor principalities, nor powers, nor things present, nor things to come, ³⁹ Nor height, nor depth, nor any other creature, shall be able to separate us from the love of God, which is in Christ Jesus our Lord." (Romans 8:38-39)

128. "Behold, I stand at the door, and knock: if any man hear my voice, and open the door, I will come in to him, and will sup with him, and he with me." (Revelation 3:20)

129. "Wait on the LORD: be of good courage, and he shall strengthen thine heart: wait, I say, on the LORD." (Psalm 27:14)

130. "'No weapon that is formed against thee shall prosper; and every tongue that shall rise against thee in judgment thou shalt condemn. This is the heritage of the servants of the LORD, and their righteousness is of me, saith the LORD'." (Isaiah 54:17)

131. "³ Through wisdom is a house builded; and by understanding it is established: ⁴ And by knowledge shall the chambers be filled with all precious and pleasant riches." (Proverbs 24:3-4)

132. "A faithful man shall abound with blessings: but he that maketh haste to be rich shall not be innocent." (Proverbs 28:20)

133. "He that is of a proud heart stirreth up strife: but he that putteth his trust in the LORD shall be made fat." (Proverbs 28:25)

134. "If ye be willing and obedient, ye shall eat the good of the land." (Isaiah 1:19)

135. "I will go before thee, and make the crooked places straight: I will break in pieces the gates of brass, and cut in sunder the bars of iron." (Isaiah 45:2)

136. "Thus saith the LORD, thy Redeemer, the Holy One of Israel; 'I am the LORD thy God which teacheth thee to profit, which leadeth thee by the way that thou shouldest go'." (Isaiah 48:17)

137. "But ye shall be named the Priests of the LORD: men shall call you the Ministers of our God: ye shall eat the riches of the Gentiles, and in their glory shall ye boast yourselves." (Isaiah 61:6)

138. "For your shame ye shall have double; and for confusion they shall rejoice in their portion: therefore in their land they shall possess the double: everlasting joy shall be unto them." (Isaiah 61:7)

139. "When thy wares went forth out of the seas, thou filledst many people; thou didst enrich the kings of the earth with the multitude of thy riches and of thy merchandise." (Ezekiel 27:33)

140. "For the seed shall be prosperous; the vine shall give her fruit, and the ground shall give her increase, and the heavens shall give their dew; and I will cause the remnant of this people to possess all these things." (Zechariah 8:12)

141. "And he hath brought us into this place, and hath given us this land, even a land that floweth with milk and honey." (Deuteronomy 26:9)

142. "And the LORD shall make thee plenteous in goods, in the fruit of thy body, and in the fruit of thy cattle, and in the fruit of thy ground, in the land which the LORD sware unto thy fathers to give thee." (Deuteronomy 28:11)

143. "The LORD shall open unto thee his good treasure, the heaven to give the rain unto thy land in his season, and to bless all the work of thine hand: and thou shalt lend unto many nations, and thou shalt not borrow." (Deuteronomy 28:12)

144. "And the LORD shall make thee the head, and not the tail; and thou shalt be above only, and thou shalt not be beneath; if that thou hearken unto the commandments of the LORD thy God, which I command thee this day, to observe and to do them." (Deuteronomy 28:13)

145. "Keep therefore the words of this covenant, and do them, that ye may prosper in all that ye do." (Deuteronomy 29:9)

146. "And the LORD thy God will make thee plenteous in every work of thine hand, in the fruit of thy body, and in the fruit of thy cattle, and in the fruit of thy land, for good: for the LORD will again rejoice over thee for good, as he rejoiced over thy fathers." (Deuteronomy 30:9)

147. "¹⁵ See, I have set before thee this day, life and good, and death and evil; ¹⁶ In that I command thee this day to love the LORD thy God, to walk in his ways, and to keep his commandments and his statutes and his judgments, that thou mayest live and multiply: and the LORD thy God shall bless thee in the land whither thou goest to possess it." (Deuteronomy 30:15-16)

148. "And Judah also shall fight at Jerusalem; and the wealth of all the heathen round about shall be gathered together, gold, and silver, and apparel, in great abundance." (Zechariah 14:14)

149. "'And all nations shall call you blessed: for ye shall be a delight-some land,' saith the LORD of hosts." (Malachi 3:12)

150. "I will hear what God the LORD will speak: for he will speak peace unto his people, and to his saints: but let them not turn again to folly." (Psalm 85:8)

151. "Neither was there any among them that lacked: for as many as were possessors of lands or houses sold them, and brought the prices of the things that were sold." (Act 4:34)

152. "Owe no man anything, but to love one another: for he that loveth another hath fulfilled the law." (Romans 13:8)

153. "And God is able to make all grace abound toward you; that ye, always having all sufficiency in all things, may abound to every good work." (2 Corinthians 9:8)

154. "Being enriched in everything to all bountifulness, which causeth through us thanksgiving to God." (2 Corinthians 9:11)

155. "That the blessing of Abraham might come on the Gentiles through Jesus Christ; that we might receive the promise of the Spirit through faith." (Galatians 3:14)

156. "Be not deceived; God is not mocked: for whatsoever a man soweth, that shall he also reap." (Galatians 6:7)

157. "But my God shall supply all your need according to his riches in glory by Christ Jesus." (Philippians 4:19)

158. "Charge them that are rich in this world, that they be not high-minded, nor trust in uncertain riches, but in the living God, who giveth us richly all things to enjoy." (1 Timothy 6:17)

159. "That they do good, that they be rich in good works, ready to distribute, willing to communicate." (1 Timothy 6:18)

160. "And if ye be Christ's, then are ye Abraham's seed, and heirs according to the promise." (Galatians 3:29)

161. "The LORD preserveth the strangers; he relieveth the fatherless and widow: but the way of the wicked he turneth upside down." (Psalm 146:9)

162. "Thou wilt keep him in perfect peace, whose mind is stayed on thee: because he trusteth in thee." (Isaiah 26:3)

163. "For ye shall go out with joy, and be led forth with peace: the mountains and the hills shall break forth before you into singing, and all the trees of the field shall clap their hands." (Isaiah 55:12)

164. "For it is God which worketh in you both to will and to do of his good pleasure." (Philippians 2:13)

165. "The LORD is merciful and gracious, slow to anger, and plenteous in mercy." (Psalm 103:8)

166. "¹³ And it shall come to pass, if ye shall hearken diligently unto my commandments, which I command you this day, to love the LORD your God, and to serve him with all your heart and with all your soul, ¹⁴ That I will give you the rain of your land in his due season, the first rain and the latter rain, that thou mayest gather in thy corn, and thy wine, and thine oil." (Deuteronomy 11:13-14)

167. "The LORD is good, a strong hold in the day of trouble; and he knoweth them that trust in him." (Nahum 1:7)

168. "For the eyes of the LORD run to and fro throughout the whole earth, to shew himself strong in the behalf of them whose heart is perfect toward him. Herein thou hast done foolishly: therefore from henceforth thou shalt have wars." (2 Chronicles 16:9)

169. "The Spirit of the Lord God is upon me; because the Lord hath anointed me to preach good tidings unto the meek; he hath sent me to bind up the brokenhearted, to proclaim liberty to the captives, and the opening of the prison to them that are bound." (Isaiah 61:1)

170. "[26] A new heart also will I give you, and a new spirit will I put within you: and I will take away the stony heart out of your flesh, and I will give you an heart of flesh. [27] And I will put my spirit within you, and cause you to walk in my statutes, and ye shall keep my judgments, and do them." (Ezekiel 36:26-27)

171. "If the Son therefore shall make you free, ye shall be free indeed." (John 8:36)

172. "[14] Because he hath set his love upon me, therefore will I deliver him: I will set him on high, because he hath known my name. [15] He shall call upon me, and I will answer him: I will be with him in trouble; I will deliver him, and honor him." (Psalm 91:14-15)

173. "Submit yourselves therefore to God. Resist the devil, and he will flee from you." (James 4:7)

174. "⁹ The LORD also will be a refuge for the oppressed, a refuge in times of trouble. ¹⁰ And they that know thy name will put their trust in thee: for thou, LORD, hast not forsaken them that seek thee." (Psalm 9:9-10)

175. "Honor thy father and thy mother: that thy days may be long upon the land which the LORD thy God giveth thee." (Exodus 20:12)

176. "Train up a child in the way he should go: and when he is old, he will not depart from it." (Proverbs 22:6)

177. "I will call upon the LORD, who is worthy to be praised: so shall I be saved from mine enemies." (Psalm 18:3)

178. "Yea, though I walk through the valley of the shadow of death, I will fear no evil: for thou art with me; thy rod and thy staff they comfort me." (Psalm 23:4)

179. "¹⁷ And it shall come to pass in the last days, saith God, 'I will pour out of my Spirit upon all flesh: and your sons and your daughters shall prophesy, and your young men shall see visions, and your old men shall dream dreams: ¹⁸ And on my servants and on my handmaidens I will pour out in those days of my Spirit; and they shall prophesy'." (Acts 2:17-18)

180. "³⁸ Then Peter said unto them, 'Repent, and be baptized every one of you in the name of Jesus Christ for the remission of sins, and ye shall receive the gift of the Holy Ghost. ³⁹ For the promise is unto you, and to your children, and to all that are afar off, even as many as the LORD our God shall call'." (Acts 2:38-39)

181. "Lest when thou hast eaten and art full, and hast built goodly houses, and dwelt therein." (Deuteronomy 8:12)

182. "Thou hast forgiven the iniquity of thy people, thou hast covered all their sin. Selah." (Psalm 85:2)

183. "For thou, Lord, art good, and ready to forgive; and plenteous in mercy unto all them that call upon thee." (Psalm 86:5)

184. "And when ye stand praying, forgive, if ye have ought against any: that your Father also which is in heaven may forgive you your trespasses." (Mark 11:25)

185. "And be ye kind one to another, tenderhearted, forgiving one another, even as God for Christ's sake hath forgiven you." (Ephesians 4:32)

186. "If we confess our sins, he is faithful and just to forgive us our sins, and to cleanse us from all unrighteousness." (1 John 1:9)

187. "What man is he that feareth the LORD? him shall he teach in the way that he shall choose." (Psalm 25:12)

188. "I will instruct thee and teach thee in the way which thou shalt go: I will guide thee with mine eye." (Psalm 32:8)

189. "And it shall come to pass, that before they call, I will answer; and while they are yet speaking, I will hear." (Isaiah 65:24)

190. "Howbeit when he, the Spirit of truth, is come, he will guide you into all truth: for he shall not speak of himself; but whatsoever he shall hear, that shall he speak: and he will shew you things to come." (John 16:13)

191. "² Bless the LORD, O my soul, and forget not all his benefits: ³ Who forgiveth all thine iniquities; who healeth all thy diseases; ⁴ Who redeemeth thy life from destruction; who crowneth thee with loving kindness and tender mercies; ⁵ Who satisfieth thy mouth with good things; so that thy youth is renewed like the eagle's." (Psalm 103:2-5)

192. "I have blotted out, as a thick cloud, thy transgressions, and, as a cloud, thy sins: return unto me; for I have redeemed thee." (Isaiah 44:22)

193. "And I will deliver thee out of the hand of the wicked, and I will redeem thee out of the hand of the terrible." (Jeremiah 15:21)

194. "He giveth power to the faint; and to them that have no might he increaseth strength." (Isaiah 40:29)

195. "And let us not be weary in well doing: for in due season we shall reap, if we faint not." (Galatians 6:9)

196. "The LORD is gracious, and full of compassion; slow to anger, and of great mercy." (Psalm 145:8)

197. "And the LORD shall help them, and deliver them: he shall deliver them from the wicked, and save them, because they trust in him." (Psalm 37:40)

198. "The meek shall eat and be satisfied: they shall praise the LORD that seek him: your heart shall live forever." (Psalm 22:26)

199. "And they said, 'Believe on the Lord Jesus Christ, and thou shalt be saved, and thy house'." (Acts 16:31)

200. "⁶ For the LORD giveth wisdom: out of his mouth cometh knowledge and understanding. ⁷ He layeth up sound wisdom for the righteous: he is a buckler to them that walk uprightly." (Proverbs 2:6-7)

201. "So then faith cometh by hearing, and hearing by the word of God." (Romans 10:17)

202. "For if ye turn again unto the LORD, your brethren and your children shall find compassion before them that lead them captive, so that they shall come again into this land: for the LORD your God is gracious and merciful, and will not turn away his face from you, if ye return unto him." (2 Chronicles 30:9)

203. "And thou shalt do that which is right and good in the sight of the LORD: that it may be well with thee, and that thou mayest go in and possess the good land which the LORD sware unto thy fathers." (Deuteronomy 6:18)

204. "For thou, LORD, wilt bless the righteous; with favor wilt thou compass him as with a shield." (Psalm 5:12)

205. "When thou liest down, thou shalt not be afraid: yea, thou shalt lie down, and thy sleep shall be sweet." (Proverbs 3:24)

206. "The glory of young men is their strength: and the beauty of old men is the grey head." (Proverbs 20:29)

207. "He will swallow up death in victory; and the Lord God will wipe away tears from off all faces; and the rebuke of his people shall he take away from off all the earth: for the Lord hath spoken it." (Isaiah 25:8)

208. "For sin shall not have dominion over you: for ye are not under the law, but under grace." (Romans 6:14)

209. "By humility and the fear of the Lord are riches, and honor, and life." (Proverbs 22:4)

210. "But he that shall endure unto the end, the same shall be saved." (Matthew 24:13)

211. "Every man also to whom God hath given riches and wealth, and hath given him power to eat thereof, and to take his portion, and to rejoice in his labour; this is the gift of God." (Ecclesiastes 5:19)

212. "The fear of the LORD is the beginning of knowledge: but fools despise wisdom and instruction." (Proverbs 1:7)

213. "But whoso hearkeneth unto me shall dwell safely, and shall be quiet from fear of evil." (Proverbs 1:33)

214. "⁷ Beloved, let us love one another: for love is of God; and every one that loveth is born of God, and knoweth God. ⁸ He that loveth not knoweth not God; for God is love." (1 John 4:7-8)

215. "And all things, whatsoever ye shall ask in prayer, believing, ye shall receive." (Matthew 21:22)

216. "For if these things be in you, and abound, they make you that ye shall neither be barren nor unfruitful in the knowledge of our Lord Jesus Christ." (2 Peter 1:8)

217. "For the LORD taketh pleasure in his people: he will beautify the meek with salvation." (Psalm 149:4)

218. "[24] Therefore whosoever heareth these sayings of mine, and doeth them, I will liken him unto a wise man, which built his house upon a rock: [25] And the rain descended, and the floods came, and the winds blew, and beat upon that house; and it fell not: for it was founded upon a rock." (Matthew 7:24-25)

219. "And I will send grass in thy fields for thy cattle, that thou mayest eat and be full." (Deuteronomy 11:15)

220. "[1] God is our refuge and strength, a very present help in trouble. [2] Therefore will not we fear, though the earth be removed, and though the mountains be carried into the midst of the sea." (Psalm 46:1-2)

221. "If they obey and serve him, they shall spend their days in prosperity, and their years in pleasures." (Job 36:11)

222. "[3] Trust in the LORD, and do good; so shalt thou dwell in the land, and verily thou shalt be fed. [4] Delight thyself also in the LORD: and he shall give thee the desires of thine heart. [5] Commit thy way unto the LORD; trust also in him; and he shall bring it to pass." (Psalm 37:3-5)

223. "And ye shall serve the LORD your God, and he shall bless thy bread, and thy water; and I will take sickness away from the midst of thee." (Exodus 23:25)

224. "I will abundantly bless her provision: I will satisfy her poor with bread." (Psalm 132:15)

225. "Fear not, little flock; for it is your Father's good pleasure to give you the kingdom." (Luke 12:32)

226. "⁷ The LORD shall preserve thee from all evil: he shall preserve thy soul. ⁸ The LORD shall preserve thy going out and thy coming in from this time forth, and even for evermore." (Psalm 121:7-8)

227. "If ye then, being evil, know how to give good gifts unto your children, how much more shall your Father which is in heaven give good things to them that ask him?." (Matthew 7:11)

228. "Turn you at my reproof: behold, I will pour out my spirit unto you, I will make known my words unto you." (Proverbs 1:23)

229. "And God shall wipe away all tears from their eyes; and there shall be no more death, neither sorrow, nor crying, neither shall there be any more pain: for the former things are passed away." (Revelation 21:4)

230. "And every man that hath this hope in him purifieth himself, even as he is pure." (1 John 3:3)

231. "[14] And this is the confidence that we have in him, that, if we ask any thing according to his will, he heareth us: [15] And if we know that he hear us, whatsoever we ask, we know that we have the petitions that we desired of him." (1 John 5:14-15)

232. "[34] A new commandment I give unto you, That ye love one another; as I have loved you, that ye also love one another. [35] By this shall all men know that ye are my disciples, if ye have love one to another." (John 13:34-35)

233. "[8] We are troubled on every side, yet not distressed; we are perplexed, but not in despair; [9] Persecuted, but not forsaken; cast down, but not destroyed." (2 Corinthians 4:8-9)

234. "²² It is of the Lord's mercies that we are not consumed, because his compassions fail not. ²³ They are new every morning: great is thy faithfulness. ²⁴ The Lord is my portion, saith my soul; therefore will I hope in him. ²⁵ The Lord is good unto them that wait for him, to the soul that seeketh him." (Lamentations 3:22-25)

235. "⁷ The law of the Lord is perfect, converting the soul: the testimony of the Lord is sure, making wise the simple. ⁸ The statutes of the Lord are right, rejoicing the heart: the commandment of the Lord is pure, enlightening the eyes. ⁹ The fear of the Lord is clean, enduring for ever: the judgments of the Lord are true and righteous altogether." (Psalm 19:7-9)

236. "³ And not only so, but we glory in tribulations also: knowing that tribulation worketh patience; ⁴ And patience, experience; and experience, hope: ⁵ And hope maketh not ashamed; because the love of God is shed abroad in our hearts by the Holy Ghost which is given unto us." (Romans 5:3-5)

237. "² In my Father's house are many mansions: if it were not so, I would have told you. I go to prepare a place for you. ³ And if I go and prepare a place for you, I will come again, and receive you unto myself; that where I am, there ye may be also." (John 14:2-3)

238. "To an inheritance incorruptible, and undefiled, and that fadeth not away, reserved in heaven for you." (1 Peter 1:4)

239. "¹⁶ And I will pray the Father, and he shall give you another Comforter, that he may abide with you forever; ¹⁷ Even the Spirit of truth; whom the world cannot receive, because it seeth him not, neither knoweth him: but ye know him; for he dwelleth with you, and shall be in you." (John 14:16-17)

240. "But ye are not in the flesh, but in the Spirit, if so be that the Spirit of God dwell in you. Now if any man have not the Spirit of Christ, he is none of his." (Romans 8:9)

241. "Now the Lord of peace himself give you peace always by all means. The Lord be with you all." (2 Thessalonians 3:16)

242. "And the LORD passed by before him, and proclaimed, The LORD, The LORD God, merciful and gracious, longsuffering, and abundant in goodness and truth." (Exodus 34:6)

243. "And his mercy is on them that fear him from generation to generation." (Luke 1:50)

244. "¹ I will sing of the mercies of the LORD for ever: with my mouth will I make known thy faithfulness to all generations. ² For I have said, 'Mercy shall be built up forever: thy faithfulness shalt thou establish in the very heavens'." (Psalm 89:1-2)

245. "¹⁸ Who is a God like unto thee that pardoneth iniquity, and passeth by the transgression of the remnant of his heritage? He retaineth not his anger forever, because he delighteth in mercy. ¹⁹ He will turn again, he will have compassion upon us; he will subdue our iniquities; and thou wilt cast all their sins into the depths of the sea." (Micah 7:18-19)

246. "Every word of God is pure: he is a shield unto them that put their trust in him." (Proverbs 30:5)

247. "¹⁷ The righteous cry, and the LORD heareth, and delivereth them out of all their troubles. ¹⁸ The LORD is nigh unto them that are of a broken heart; and saveth such as be of a contrite spirit." (Psalm 34:17-18)

248. "¹ The preparations of the heart in man, and the answer of the tongue, is from the LORD. ² All the ways of a man are clean in his own eyes; but the LORD weigheth the spirits. ³ Commit thy works unto the LORD, and thy thoughts shall be established." (Proverbs 16:1-3)

249. "³ What time I am afraid, I will trust in thee. ⁴ In God I will praise his word, in God I have put my trust; I will not fear what flesh can do unto me." (Psalm 56:3-4)

250. "¹³ Thou shalt fear the LORD thy God, and serve him, and shalt swear by his name. ¹⁴ Ye shall not go after other gods, of the gods of the people which are round about you." (Deuteronomy 6:13-14)

251. "But thanks be to God, which giveth us the victory through our Lord Jesus Christ." (1 Corinthians 15:57)

252. "⁷ Submit yourselves therefore to God. Resist the devil, and he will flee from you. ⁸ Draw nigh to God, and he will draw nigh to you. Cleanse your hands, ye sinners; and purify your hearts, ye double minded." (James 4:7-8)

253. "And they that know thy name will put their trust in thee: for thou, LORD, hast not forsaken them that seek thee." (Psalm 9:10)

254. "And of Benjamin he said, 'The beloved of the LORD shall dwell in safety by him; and the Lord shall cover him all the day long, and he shall dwell between his shoulders'." (Deuteronomy 33:12)

255. "Though I walk in the midst of trouble, thou wilt revive me: thou shalt stretch forth thine hand against the wrath of mine enemies, and thy right hand shall save me." (Psalm 138:7)

256. "And he will love thee, and bless thee, and multiply thee: he will also bless the fruit of thy womb, and the fruit of thy land, thy corn, and thy wine, and thine oil, the increase of thy kine, and the flocks of thy sheep, in the land which he sware unto thy fathers to give thee." (Deuteronomy 7:13)

257. "² And the people shall take them, and bring them to their place: and the house of Israel shall possess them in the land of the LORD for servants and handmaids: and they shall take them captives, whose captives they were; and they shall rule over their oppressors. ³ And it shall come to pass in the day that the LORD shall give thee rest from thy sorrow, and from thy fear, and from the hard bondage wherein thou wast made to serve." (Isaiah 14:2-3)

258.   "²⁹ And he said unto them, 'Verily I say unto you, There is no man that hath left house, or parents, or brethren, or wife, or children, for the kingdom of God's sake, ³⁰ Who shall not receive manifold more in this present time, and in the world to come life everlasting'." (Luke 18:29-30)

259.   "²² And Jesus answering saith unto them, 'Have faith in God.' ²³ For verily I say unto you, 'That whosoever shall say unto this mountain, Be thou removed, and be thou cast into the sea; and shall not doubt in his heart, but shall believe that those things which he saith shall come to pass; he shall have whatsoever he saith'." (Mark 11:22-23)

260.   "He that hath my commandments, and keepeth them, he it is that loveth me: and he that loveth me shall be loved of my Father, and I will love him, and will manifest myself to him." (John 14:21)

261.   "In whom we have redemption through his blood, the forgiveness of sins, according to the riches of his grace." (Ephesians 1:7)

262. "My covenant will I not break, nor alter the thing that is gone out of my lips." (Psalm 89:34)

263. "And this is the promise that he hath promised us, even eternal life." (1 John 2:25)

264. "But thus saith the LORD, Even the captives of the mighty shall be taken away, and the prey of the terrible shall be delivered: for I will contend with him that contendeth with thee, and I will save thy children." (Isaiah 49:25)

265. "Thou wilt keep him in perfect peace, whose mind is stayed on thee: because he trusteth in thee." (Isaiah 26:3)

266. "There hath no temptation taken you but such as is common to man: but God is faithful, who will not suffer you to be tempted above that ye are able; but will with the temptation also make a way to escape, that ye may be able to bear it." (1 Corinthians 10:13)

267. "O give thanks unto the LORD; for he is good; for his mercy endureth for ever." (1 Chronicles 16:34)

268. "² Blessed is the man that walketh not in the counsel of the ungodly, nor standeth in the way of sinners, nor sitteth in the seat of the scornful. ² But his delight is in the law of the LORD; and in his law doth he meditate day and night. ³ And he shall be like a tree planted by the rivers of water, that bringeth forth his fruit in his season; his leaf also shall not wither; and whatsoever he doeth shall prosper." (Psalm 1:1-3)

269. "¹⁶ For I am not ashamed of the gospel of Christ: for it is the power of God unto salvation to everyone that believeth; to the Jew first, and also to the Greek. ¹⁷ For therein is the righteousness of God revealed from faith to faith: as it is written, the just shall live by faith." (Romans 1:16-17)

270. "And thine ears shall hear a word behind thee, saying, This is the way, walk ye in it, when ye turn to the right hand, and when ye turn to the left." (Isaiah 30:21)

271. "(For we walk by faith, not by sight:)." (2 Corinthians 5:7)

272. "¹ Children, obey your parents in the Lord: for this is right. ² Honor thy father and mother; which is the first commandment with promise; ³That it may be well with thee, and thou mayest live long on the earth." (Ephesians 6:1-3)

273. "Great peace have they which love thy law: and nothing shall offend them." (Psalm 119:165)

274. ¹² And whosoever shall exalt himself shall be abased; and he that shall humble himself shall be exalted. (Matthew 23:12)

275. "For I reckon that the sufferings of this present time are not worthy to be compared with the glory which shall be revealed in us." (Romans 8:18)

276. "⁹ After this manner therefore pray ye: Our Father which art in heaven, Hallowed be thy name. ¹⁰ Thy kingdom come, Thy will be done in earth, as it is in heaven. ¹¹ Give us this day our daily bread. ¹² And forgive us our debts, as we forgive our debtors. ¹³ And lead us not into temptation, but deliver us from evil: For thine is the kingdom, and the power, and the glory, forever. Amen." (Matthew 6:9-13)

277. "I have been young, and now am old; yet have I not seen the righteous forsaken, nor his seed begging bread. (Psalm 37:25)

278. "For this is the love of God, that we keep his commandments: and his commandments are not grievous." (1 John 5:3)

279. "But if from thence thou shalt seek the LORD thy God, thou shalt find him, if thou seek him with all thy heart and with all thy soul." (Deuteronomy 4:29)

280. "For what nation is there so great, who hath God so nigh unto them, as the LORD our God is in all things that we call upon him for?." (Deuteronomy 4:7)

281. "⁵ And beside this, giving all diligence, add to your faith virtue; and to virtue knowledge; ⁶ And to knowledge temperance; and to temperance patience; and to patience godliness; ⁷ And to godliness brotherly kindness; and to brotherly kindness charity. ⁸ For if these things be in you, and abound, they make you that ye shall neither be barren nor unfruitful in the knowledge of our Lord Jesus Christ." (2 Peter 1:5-8)

282. "And Jesus said unto them, 'Because of your unbelief: for verily I say unto you, If ye have faith as a grain of mustard seed, ye shall say unto this mountain, Remove hence to yonder place; and it shall remove; and nothing shall be impossible unto you.'" (Matthew 17:20)

283. "'Verily, verily,' I say unto you, 'He that heareth my word, and believeth on him that sent me, hath everlasting life, and shall not come into condemnation; but is passed from death unto life.'" (John 5:24)

284. "That if thou shalt confess with thy mouth the Lord Jesus, and shalt believe in thine heart that God hath raised him from the dead, thou shalt be saved." (Romans 10:9)

285. "Unto the woman he said, 'I will greatly multiply thy sorrow and thy conception; in sorrow thou shalt bring forth children; and thy desire shall be to thy husband, and he shall rule over thee.'" (Genesis 3:16)

286. "But whosoever drinketh of the water that I shall give him shall never thirst; but the water that I shall give him shall be in him a well of water springing up into everlasting life." (John 4:14)

287. "And I give unto them eternal life; and they shall never perish, neither shall any man pluck them out of my hand." (John 10:28)

288. "In every thing give thanks: for this is the will of God in Christ Jesus concerning you." (1 Thessalonians 5:18)

289. "Blessed be the God and Father of our Lord Jesus Christ, who hath blessed us with all spiritual blessings in heavenly places in Christ." (Ephesians 1:3)

290. "Being confident of this very thing, that he which hath begun a good work in you will perform it until the day of Jesus Christ." (Philippians 1:6)

291. "Behold the fowls of the air: for they sow not, neither do they reap, nor gather into barns; yet your heavenly Father feedeth them. Are ye not much better than they?." (Matthew 6:26)

292. "He that covereth his sins shall not prosper: but whoso confesseth and forsaketh them shall have mercy." (Proverbs 28:13)

293. "³¹ The ear that heareth the reproof of life abideth among the wise. ³² He that refuseth instruction despiseth his own soul: but he that heareth reproof getteth understanding." (Proverbs 15:31-32)

294. "¹² Put on therefore, as the elect of God, holy and beloved, bowels of mercies, kindness, humbleness of mind, meekness, longsuffering; ¹³ Forbearing one another, and forgiving one another, if any man have a quarrel against any: even as Christ forgave you, so also do ye." (Colossians 3:12-13)

295. "In hope of eternal life, which God, that cannot lie, promised before the world began." (Titus 1:2)

296. "[13] For when God made promise to Abraham, because he could swear by no greater, he sware by himself, [14] Saying, Surely blessing I will bless thee, and multiplying I will multiply thee. [15] And so, after he had patiently endured, he obtained the promise. [16] For men verily swear by the greater: and an oath for confirmation is to them an end of all strife. [17] Wherein God, willing more abundantly to shew unto the heirs of promise the immutability of his counsel, confirmed it by an oath: [18] That by two immutable things, in which it was impossible for God to lie, we might have a strong consolation, who have fled for refuge to lay hold upon the hope set before us." (Hebrews 6:13-18)

297. "But unto you that fear my name shall the Sun of righteousness arise with healing in his wings; and ye shall go forth, and grow up as calves of the stall." (Malachi 4:2)

298. "So shall my word be that goeth forth out of my mouth: it shall not return unto me void, but it shall accomplish that which I please, and it shall prosper in the thing whereto I sent it." (Isaiah 55:11)

299. "And being fully persuaded that, what he had promised, he was able also to perform." (Romans 4:21)

300. "[17] That the God of our Lord Jesus Christ, the Father of glory, may give unto you the spirit of wisdom and revelation in the knowledge of him: [18] The eyes of your understanding being enlightened; that ye may know what is the hope of his calling, and what the riches of the glory of his inheritance in the saints." (Ephesians 1:17-18)

301. "The thoughts of the wicked are an abomination to the LORD: but the words of the pure are pleasant words." (Proverbs 15:26)

302. "[8] The wisdom of the prudent is to understand his way: but the folly of fools is deceit. [9] Fools make a mock at sin: but among the righteous there is favour." (Proverbs 14:8-9)

303. "I am that bread of life." (John 6:48)

304. "The LORD thy God in the midst of thee is mighty; he will save, he will rejoice over thee with joy; he will rest in his love, he will joy over thee with singing." (Zephaniah 3:17)

305. "[17] For the arms of the wicked shall be broken: but the LORD upholdeth the righteous. [18] The LORD knoweth the days of the upright: and their inheritance shall be forever. [19] They shall not be ashamed in the evil time: and in the days of famine they shall be satisfied." (Psalm 37:17-19)

306. "[13] For thou hast possessed my reins: thou hast covered me in my mother's womb. [14] I will praise thee; for I am fearfully and wonderfully made: marvelous are thy works; and that my soul knoweth right well." (Psalm 139:13-14)

307. "If ye abide in me, and my words abide in you, ye shall ask what ye will, and it shall be done unto you." (John 15:7)

308. "[12] And I will walk among you, and will be your God, and ye shall be my people. [13] I am the LORD your God, which brought you forth out of the land of Egypt, that ye should not be their bondmen; and I have broken the bands of your yoke, and made you go upright." (Leviticus 26:12-13)

309. "He that believeth and is baptized shall be saved; but he that believeth not shall be damned." (Mark 16:16)

310. "²² Ye shall not fear them: for the LORD your God he shall fight for you." (Deuteronomy 3:22)

311. "My sheep hear my voice, and I know them, and they follow me." (John 10:27)

312. "And we know that all things work together for good to them that love God, to them who are the called according to his purpose." (Romans 8:28)

313. "For the promise, that he should be the heir of the world, was not to Abraham, or to his seed, through the law, but through the righteousness of faith." (Romans 4:13)

314. "Then spake Jesus again unto them, saying, I am the light of the world: he that followeth me shall not walk in darkness, but shall have the light of life." (John 8:12)

315. "Jesus said unto her, 'I am the resurrection, and the life: he that believeth in me, though he were dead, yet shall he live'." (John 11:25)

316. "There failed not ought of any good thing which the LORD had spoken unto the house of Israel; all came to pass." (Joshua 21:45)

317. "Thy kingdom is an everlasting kingdom, and thy dominion endureth throughout all generations." (Psalm 145:13)

318. "Let us hold fast the profession of our faith without wavering; (for he is faithful that promised;)." (Hebrews 10:23)

319. "And for this cause he is the mediator of the new testament, that by means of death, for the redemption of the transgressions that were under the first testament, they which are called might receive the promise of eternal inheritance." (Hebrews 9:15)

320. "Think not that I am come to destroy the law, or the prophets: I am not come to destroy, but to fulfill." (Matthew 5:17)

321. "And ye are complete in him, which is the head of all principality and power." (Colossians 2:10)

322. "Even when we were dead in sins, hath quickened us together with Christ, (by grace ye are saved;)." (Ephesians 2:5)

323. "For the law of the Spirit of life in Christ Jesus hath made me free from the law of sin and death." (Romans 8:2)

324. "In righteousness shalt thou be established: thou shalt be far from oppression; for thou shalt not fear: and from terror; for it shall not come near thee." (Isaiah 54:14)

325. "Ye are of God, little children, and have overcome them: because greater is he that is in you, than he that is in the world." (1 John 4:4)

326. "For if by one man's offence death reigned by one; much more they which receive abundance of grace and of the gift of righteousness shall reign in life by one, Jesus Christ." (Romans 5:17)

327. "¹⁷ And these signs shall follow them that believe; In my name shall they cast out devils; they shall speak with new tongues; ¹⁸ They shall take up serpents; and if they drink any deadly thing, it shall not hurt them; they shall lay hands on the sick, and they shall recover." (Mark 16:17-18)

328. "⁹ Lie not one to another, seeing that ye have put off the old man with his deeds; ¹⁰ And have put on the new man, which is renewed in knowledge after the image of him that created him." (Colossians 3:9-10)

329. "Above all, taking the shield of faith, wherewith ye shall be able to quench all the fiery darts of the wicked." (Ephesians 6:16)

330. "² My brethren, count it all joy when ye fall into diverse temptations; ³ Knowing this, that the trying of your faith worketh patience. ⁴ But let patience have her perfect work, that ye may be perfect and entire, wanting nothing." (James 1:2-4)

331. "¹² For there is no difference between the Jew and the Greek: for the same Lord over all is rich unto all that call upon him. ¹³ For whosoever shall call upon the name of the Lord shall be saved." (Romans 10:12-13)

332. "¹¹And the Lᴏʀᴅ shall guide thee continually, and satisfy thy soul in drought, and make fat thy bones: and thou shalt be like a watered garden, and like a spring of water, whose waters fail not." (Isaiah 58:11)

333. "And I say also unto thee, That thou art Peter, and upon this rock I will build my church; and the gates of hell shall not prevail against it." (Matthew 16:18)

334. "He that walketh with wise men shall be wise: but a companion of fools shall be destroyed." (Proverbs 13:20)

335. "But ye are a chosen generation, a royal priesthood, an holy nation, a peculiar people; that ye should shew forth the praises of him who hath called you out of darkness into his marvelous light." (1 Peter 2:9)

336. "³The God of my rock; in him will I trust: he is my shield, and the horn of my salvation, my high tower, and my refuge, my saviour; thou savest me from violence. ⁴I will call on the Lᴏʀᴅ, who is worthy to be praised: so shall I be saved from mine enemies." (2 Samuel 22:3-4)

337. "Many are the afflictions of the righteous: but the Lord delivereth him out of them all." (Psalm 34:19)

338. "A thousand shall fall at thy side, and ten thousand at thy right hand; but it shall not come nigh thee." (Psalm 91:7)

339. "These things I have spoken unto you, that in me ye might have peace. In the world ye shall have tribulation: but be of good cheer; I have overcome the world." (John 16:33)

340. "These things have I spoken unto you, that my joy might remain in you, and that your joy might be full." (John 15:11)

341. "Seeing then that we have a great high priest, that is passed into the heavens, Jesus the Son of God, let us hold fast our profession." (Hebrews 4:14)

342. "⁵ Let your conversation be without covetousness; and be content with such things as ye have: for he hath said, 'I will never leave thee, nor forsake thee.' ⁶ So that we may boldly say, 'The Lord is my helper, and I will not fear what man shall do unto me.'" (Hebrews 13:5-6)

343. "Behold, I come quickly: hold that fast which thou hast, that no man take thy crown." (Revelation 3:11)

344. "All that the Father giveth me shall come to me; and him that cometh to me I will in no wise cast out." (John 6:37)

345. "Be strong and of a good courage, fear not, nor be afraid of them: for the LORD thy God, he it is that doth go with thee; he will not fail thee, nor forsake thee." (Deuteronomy 31:6)

346. "The angel of the LORD encampeth round about them that fear him, and delivereth them." (Psalm 34:7)

347. "And the Spirit and the bride say, "Come." And let him that heareth say, "Come." And let him that is athirst come. And whosoever will, let him take the water of life freely." (Revelation 22:17)

348. "Draw nigh to God, and he will draw nigh to you. Cleanse your hands, ye sinners; and purify your hearts, ye double minded." (James 4:8)

349. "Nevertheless we, according to his promise, look for new heavens and a new earth, wherein dwelleth righteousness." (2 Peter 3:13)

350. "Whosoever believeth that Jesus is the Christ is born of God: and every one that loveth him that begat loveth him also that is begotten of him." (1 John 5:1)

351. "Behold the fowls of the air: for they sow not, neither do they reap, nor gather into barns; yet your heavenly Father feedeth them. Are ye not much better than they?." (Matthew 6:26)

352. "²⁴ Now unto him that is able to keep you from falling, and to present you faultless before the presence of his glory with exceeding joy, ²⁵ To the only wise God our Saviour, be glory and majesty, dominion and power, both now and ever. Amen." (Jude 1:24-25)

353. "Blessed is he that readeth, and they that hear the words of this prophecy, and keep those things which are written therein: for the time is at hand." (Revelation 1:3)

354. "Rooted and built up in him, and established in the faith, as ye have been taught, abounding therein with thanksgiving." (Colossians 2:7)

355. "Submit yourselves therefore to God. Resist the devil, and he will flee from you." (James 4:7)

356. "Strengthened with all might, according to his glorious power, unto all patience and longsuffering with joyfulness." (Colossians 1:11)

357. "¹⁸ And Jesus came and spake unto them, saying, All power is given unto me in heaven and in earth. ¹⁹ Go ye therefore, and teach all nations, baptizing them in the name of the Father, and of the Son, and of the Holy Ghost: ²⁰ Teaching them to observe all things whatsoever I have commanded you: and, lo, I am with you always, even unto the end of the world. Amen." (Matthew 28:18-20)

358. "Blessed are they which do hunger and thirst after righteousness: for they shall be filled." (Matthew 5:6)

359. "And I will take you to me for a people, and I will be to you a God: and ye shall know that I am the LORD your God, which bringeth you out from under the burdens of the Egyptians." (Exodus 6:7)

360. "Thou shalt bring them in, and plant them in the mountain of thine inheritance, in the place, O LORD, which thou hast made for thee to dwell in, in the Sanctuary, O LORD, which thy hands have established." (Exodus 15:17)

361. "⁵ Now therefore, if ye will obey my voice indeed, and keep my covenant, then ye shall be a peculiar treasure unto me above all people: for all the earth is mine: ⁶ And ye shall be unto me a kingdom of priests, and a holy nation. These are the words which thou shalt speak unto the children of Israel." (Exodus 19:5-6)

362. "I am the LORD your God, which brought you out of the land of Egypt, to be your God: I am the LORD your God." (Numbers 15:41)

363. "The LORD recompense thy work, and a full reward be given thee of the LORD God of Israel, under whose wings thou art come to trust." (Ruth 2:12)

364. "⁶ And he said unto me, 'It is done. I am Alpha and Omega, the beginning and the end. I will give unto him that is athirst of the fountain of the water of life freely. ⁷ He that overcometh shall inherit all things; and I will be his God, and he shall be my son.'" (Revelation 21:6-7)

365. "⁷ For the LORD thy God hath blessed thee in all the works of thy hand: he knoweth thy walking through this great wilderness: these forty years the LORD thy God hath been with thee; thou hast lacked nothing." (Deuteronomy 2:7)

www.ingramcontent.com/pod-product-compliance
Lightning Source LLC
Chambersburg PA
CBHW071216120626
46546CB00006B/2594